NEW Spira[...] N-FICTION

Over the Wall

Bill Ridgway

Published in 2002 by:
Nelson Thornes Ltd
Delta Place
27 Bath Road
CHELTENHAM
GL53 7TH
United Kingdom

02 03 04 05 06 / 10 9 8 7 6 5 4 3 2 1

A catalogue record for this book is available from the British Library

ISBN 0-7487-6686-3

Cover illustration by Jim Eldridge
Page make-up by Tech-Set, Gateshead

Printed in Croatia by Zrinski

Introduction

Berlin is the capital of Germany. After the Second World War the city was split into two parts. The USA, Britain and France had West Berlin and Russia had East Berlin.

The Russians wanted to rule East Berlin in a different way to West Berlin. They wanted more say in how people lived their lives.

Many people in East Berlin left for the West because things were better there. By 1961 more than 2,000 East Berliners were leaving the Russian zone every day. The Russians were losing their best workers.

The Russians decided to build a wall to stop people getting out. This was called the Berlin Wall. But there were still some people who took the risk and made it to West Berlin.

This story is about a family who did just that.

1

It was early morning. Only a few people were about. Heinz felt the patter of rain and pulled up his coat collar. He took a short cut down an entry between two blocks of flats. The wind blew a torn newspaper against his legs. It was going to be another cold, wet day in East Berlin.

He turned into the street. A car came past. Then a newspaper delivery boy on his bike. It was a day like any other. On days like this Heinz felt there was nothing to look forward to.

He tried to put his sad thoughts out of his mind. He had a job, didn't he? He had a flat, and people to say 'Hello' to?

That was part of the problem. There were a lot of people to say 'Hello' to, but none of them were friends. Not here, in East Berlin. His friends had been lucky. They'd got to West Berlin before the Russians put up the Berlin Wall. There were no grey skies in West Berlin. No grey blocks and empty streets. West Berlin was alive.

But Heinz was too late. The Wall had been built. Now he was trapped. There was nothing he could do about it.

He gave a sigh and walked on. Around the corner was the place where he worked. It was called the Ministeries House. He was the odd-job man. Mr Fixit. They trusted him to keep everything working.

The Ministeries House was like any other block in East Berlin. But one thing was different. Ministeries House was right next to the Wall.

2

It would be good to see his friends in the West again. But he'd never get a pass from the guards. In the past it had been easy to cross from East to West. All you had to do was fill in a form and drive through a checkpoint.

Now anyone who wanted to cross to the West had to have a very good reason. Heinz didn't have a very good reason. If he said he wanted to see his friends again, the guards would laugh. If he told them he wanted to start a new life in the West, they'd get angry. The only way out was to escape over the Berlin Wall.

The guards were always on the lookout. You could end up in jail or even being shot for trying to get over the Wall. But it was the only way.

'If you want something badly, you can make it happen,' Heinz thought. What he wanted was a plan to get into West Berlin without getting caught. His wife and son would have to come too. He couldn't leave them behind.

He had to come up with a plan to get the three of them over the Wall. As soon as he got to West Berlin his friends would help him find work. The problem was thinking up a way to escape.

He made up his mind. He'd find a way to get out, no matter what. He'd say nothing to anyone. Not until he was ready. And while he was thinking up a plan, he'd go to work at the Ministeries House as usual.

There was always someone who'd tell the guards if they thought someone else was planning to escape. From now on he'd always be thinking of a way over the Wall. But no one would know what he was thinking . . .

No one had started work yet. Apart from the night caretaker, the Ministeries House was empty. Heinz jangled his keys and hummed a tune. If the caretaker heard him he'd say, 'That must be Heinz. Happy, as usual.'

He went down some steps and unlocked the door to a small room. The cleaners kept their brushes and buckets there. Heinz also had his workbench in the room. He kept some of his tools in a cupboard there. A vice was fixed to the bench. There was a stove for tea and a sink for washing mugs. There was stuff everywhere.

He put his bag on the workbench and lit the stove. He made himself a mug of strong tea. It would soon be time to start work.

3

He was washing up his mug when the night caretaker came in.

'I'm just clocking off,' said the caretaker.

Heinz put his mug on the side to dry. 'Any problems?' he asked.

'Just one thing,' said the caretaker. 'My TV's not working well. Could you take a look?'

Heinz had to keep the caretaker happy. Now he'd decided to escape, he had to keep people on his side. 'No problem,' Heinz smiled.

'It's just the picture,' said the caretaker. 'It's fuzzy. The sound's fine.'

'I'll check it out,' said Heinz. 'There was some wind last night. It might have blown the aerial around.'

The night caretaker left. Heinz looked through the small, dirty window. He saw the caretaker riding his bike up the street.

Heinz looked at the list of jobs he had to do. People expected him to fix things there and then. Today there were two locks to be changed. A window to mend. And there was a leak in one of the rooms. Rain was coming in from the flat roof. He took his list down from the wall and added 'Caretaker's TV'.

He took his screwdriver and some spare locks from his cupboard and went out. Five minutes later the first worker arrived. She called 'Good Morning' as she passed him. Soon other workers showed up. The building began to fill. Heinz finished changing the locks and went to see if he could mend the caretaker's TV.

It was against the rules to have a TV in your office. Heinz knew the caretaker hid it under his table. It only came out at night, when everyone else had gone home.

Heinz spent some time trying to find out what was wrong. The picture was no better when he'd finished. He decided to go on to the roof and look at the aerial.

The office staff were not allowed to go on to the roof. But Heinz was Mr Fixit. He went on to the roof every week to check the aerials and masts and to make sure the water tank was all right. There was a narrow stairway to the top. It came out through a door in the middle of a wide, flat space.

It was still raining. He began to check the aerials and masts. One of the aerials was pointing the wrong way. He moved it back and tightened the nut. Then he went over to the part of the roof that had a leak. He'd have to repair the hole to stop the water coming through.

From the roof he could see West Berlin. He moved to the edge and looked down. The Berlin Wall cut a line through the blocks of flats below him. A barbed-wire fence ran along the top. On the other side was a strip of wasteland. At night the Wall and wasteland were lit up.

Heinz was about to go back inside when he caught sight of one of the masts. It was made of criss-cross steel bars. He'd seen it a thousand times before.

But this time was different. This time an idea sprang into his mind. He had his escape plan.

4

The plan was suddenly there in his head. But it was not a full plan. He needed to work on the details. It might take some time. He had to keep calm. There were guards everywhere.

The rest of the day he worked through his list of jobs. When the time came to go home, he rang the woman who lived next to them. Heinz and his wife didn't have a phone of their own. He asked the woman to tell his wife he'd be late home.

The office workers finished for the day. Heinz sat in his workshop in the empty building with a sheet of paper and a pencil. It was getting dark outside, but he didn't want to put the light on. He didn't want anyone to know he was still in his workshop.

He drew a simple diagram. He drew it six times before he got it right. Then he made some notes by the side. By the time he'd finished it was dark outside. He heard the night caretaker come into the block. He folded his sheet of paper and put it in his pocket. Then he put on his coat to go home.

'You're late leaving,' said the caretaker as they passed.

‘Too much work, not enough pay,’ joked Heinz.

‘Did you fix my TV?’

‘Yes. It was the aerial, like I said.’

The caretaker grinned and called ‘Goodnight’.

Heinz wanted time to think. He began to walk home. The sky had cleared and a faint moon hung over the dark streets. He was wondering about his friends in West Berlin. When his plan was ready he’d need their help. He’d have to think of a way to ask them without the guards finding out.

As he got nearer home, he saw a woman taking her washing off the line. She saw Heinz, then went inside. Heinz smiled to himself. Seeing the washing line had helped him with his plan.

5

Heinz kept his eyes open for the things he needed to escape. In his workshop at the Ministeries House he kept all sorts of things that might come in handy in his job. Nuts, bolts, bits of wire, wood and paint.

He often worked at his bench. If anyone came by to ask him to fix something, they'd see all sorts of stuff lying about. Everything he needed for his escape could be kept in his workshop. No one would notice. They'd think he needed the things for his job.

In the morning he went on to the roof again. He took some tools to help him mend the leak. He looked as if he was hard at work, but really he was checking things out.

The first thing he did was check how far it was between the roof and West Berlin. He had to guess. He spent some time thinking about it, then wrote a number on his plan.

The next thing he did was check the criss-cross mast. If anyone saw him, they'd think he was inspecting it. He tested the steel bars and looked for a place where he could fix a cable.

He made a mark on the mast. This would tell him where to fix the cable. No one would ever notice the mark. They let no one else go on to the roof anyway. Only Heinz. Mr Fixit.

As he worked through the day, he kept his eyes open for other things he'd need. When the others had gone home, he spent time looking through his workshop. He had so much stuff. A lot of it was just junk.

Behind a big oil can he came across a strong rope. He laid it on the floor and measured it, two metres at a time. It was just what he needed.

He put the rope back behind the can. In an old tool box he found a hammer. That was something else he'd need.

He felt things were coming together. He'd done his sums and marked the place on the tower to fix a cable. He'd found some good rope and a hammer. He'd done the easy bit.

The rest would be much harder.

6

Heinz tried to act normally. His wife noticed he was quiet. He said he was just tired.

He was reading about a bus driver who'd tried to smash his bus through a checkpoint on the Wall. There were twelve escapers on the bus. It had been hit by a hail of bullets. Some people onboard had been killed.

Reading about the bus made him remember how risky it was trying to escape to West Berlin. He wondered if he'd end up dead when he tried. He worried about his wife and son. Would they end up being shot too?

Yet some people had got away with it. They'd hidden in cars and crawled through tunnels. A few had even leapt to safety. Maybe he'd be lucky like them. He had to be lucky for the sake of his family.

He stayed up late that night, thinking. He must have fallen asleep. When he awoke it was 2.30am. The hands on his watch glowed green in the dark. Suddenly he had the answer to another problem. He had to get some paint that would glow in the dark.

Next Saturday he had the afternoon off work. He told his wife he was going into the city for an hour or two.

He went into a toy shop. 'Do you sell paint that glows in the dark?' he asked the girl. 'My son has a toy. He wants it painted in that kind of paint. I said I'd do it for him.'

The girl shook her head. 'I know what you mean. We don't have any at the moment. But I can get you some.'

'That'll be fine. I'll call again next Saturday.'

He left the shop. He felt as if everyone knew he was planning to escape. Even the girl in the shop. But it was all in his mind. East Berlin was a big place. To the girl he was just another face.

He got on a tram. It clanged through the streets. He looked through the window at the shoppers. People got on and off. At last there were no more tall buildings. The tram was coming to the edge of the city.

He got off at the next stop. There were low blocks of flats with children playing in the street. Between the flats were old garages and untidy bits of land. Heinz walked down the street until he came to a track. He walked on by a rusty fence. Behind it were scrap cars. There was a noise of men working.

He went into the scrapyard and over to a big heap of metal parts. There were engines, steel bars and sheets of metal. He began to look through the jumble of bits and pieces.

He'd told his wife he wouldn't be long. He was just about to give up when he found what he was looking for.

7

Three weeks later, Heinz was in his workshop at the Ministeries House. He'd taken the three pulleys he'd found in the scrapyard and put them on the shelf with the hammer and the other clutter. The rope was still behind the oil can on the top shelf.

The first part of his escape plan was nearly over. But everything seemed to be taking such a long time. He wanted to move fast, but he didn't want to make mistakes. He'd have to ask someone to help him. The only person he could trust was his wife.

Heinz had said nothing to her about his plan. But his mind was made up. If she helped him make the last things he needed, they could be in West Berlin in a week or so.

That night he checked his son was asleep and closed the bedroom door quietly.

'I've got something to tell you.'

His wife looked up at him.

'I've been getting back late from work, and I know I've been quiet. It's because I've been thinking a lot.'

'About us?' asked his wife, worried.

'Yes. About us. About the three of us getting out.'

'Getting out of where? This flat?'

'Getting out of East Berlin. We're going to escape.'

'You must be mad,' she said. 'Do you want us all shot?'

'And do you want to spend the rest of your life struggling?'

Heinz was getting angry. They didn't speak for a minute. Then his wife said, 'What do you want me to do?'

'This is the plan . . .' he began.

They talked for two hours. In the end she agreed to do as he asked, and to tell no one. Not even their son.

8

Making the things took longer than he thought. First he had to draw what he wanted on paper. If the drawings were wrong he ripped them up and started again. In the end, he had a drawing that might work. His wife set about making the parts he wanted out of strips of thick cloth.

They kept the strips in the flat. Heinz didn't want to take the things she'd made to the Ministeries House yet. If anyone saw them they might think he was up to something.

As the plan came together, it was hard to keep calm. His wife was still worried about escaping. If they could get to West Berlin, they'd have a much better life. But the risk was great. What if they got caught? What would happen to their son? She hardly dared think about it. It all seemed like a dream. But it was not a dream. Each day brought danger, and a better life, one step closer.

The time came for Heinz to ask his friends on the other side of the Wall to help him. Without them, his plan wouldn't work. He had to find a way of telling them how they could help without the guards knowing.

He couldn't ask for help in a letter. Sometimes the East Berlin police read people's letters.

In the end he sent his friends a small toy. He wrote a note saying the toy was for their daughter's birthday. He said he'd like to ring to wish her Many Happy Returns.

He hoped his friends would see he had something secret to tell them. After all, they didn't have a daughter.

9

A few days later Heinz got a note from his friends in West Berlin. It said their daughter was pleased with the present he'd sent. She wanted to hear Heinz wish her Many Happy Returns. It was her birthday on Sunday. Could he ring on Sunday morning?

He was happy. His friends had understood. He'd phone them at their flat in West Berlin on Sunday. But he'd have to watch what he said. In East Berlin, it was hard to keep anything a secret.

Sunday came. He went to a phone box and rang his friends. The man in the phone office put the call through.

A woman's voice came down the line. 'Heinz? Mae was so pleased to get your present.'

'I hope it's what she wanted,' replied Heinz.

'It's just what she wanted. She's been playing with it all day. Would you like to speak to her?'

'Yes,' said Heinz. 'I'd like to wish her Many Happy Returns.'

What sounded like a little girl's voice came on the phone.

'Hello Uncle Heinz. Thank you for my present.'

'How does it feel to be four years old?'

'I'm five now,' said the voice.

'I know,' said Heinz. 'Happy Birthday. I'd like to speak to your daddy now. Could you put him on the line?'

A man's voice said, 'Heinz! Good to hear from you. How are you?'

'Fine,' said Heinz. 'I get a bit tired sometimes, but we still get out most Friday nights.'

There was a pause. Heinz hardly went anywhere. What was he trying to say?

'Do *you* still go out on Friday nights?' Heinz asked him.

Heinz was trying to tell his friend something. The friend had to play along with it.

'Yes, we still go out.'

'Where was that pub you used to go to?' asked Heinz. 'I must be getting old. I can't remember.'

Suddenly his friend knew what Heinz was saying. Heinz wanted to ring him at the pub on Friday night. The pub had a public phone.

'You want to get a doctor to look at your head,' said the friend. 'It's called the Red Rose. Remember?'

'Of course,' Heinz said. 'That's the name. I'd better ring off now. These calls are dear. Give my love to everyone. I'll be in touch.'

He put the phone down. It was early and there was no one about. He bought a paper and went back to his flat.

10

The days began to speed past. Each time Heinz phoned his friends he used a different phone box. He was still taking a risk, but it was the best he could do. They kept their talks short. He thought up ways of saying things without giving anything away. He never said 'the Ministeries House'. Instead he said 'where I work'. He never said 'the Wall'. He called it 'the problem'. He hoped anyone listening in would think he was just chatting.

Now Heinz had made his last call. He'd set the day and time of their escape. He'd got everything he needed. The only problem was how to get his wife and son into the Ministeries House without them being seen. When he'd worked out a way, his plan would be in the bag.

It was his wife who thought of a way. She'd dress up as a cleaner. She'd wear a headscarf and flat shoes and carry a bag. She could go in at night when the real cleaners were there and hide in the toilets. Heinz could draw her a plan of the Ministeries House so she'd know where to find the lavatory.

He said, 'I'll give you a spare key. In the afternoon I'll break the lavatory so it won't work. I'll put a brick in the tank. If someone asks me to mend it, I'll tell them it'll have to wait till morning. I'll tie a card on the door saying "Out of Order". Then I'll lock the door. When you come, use your key to get in and lock the door behind you. Then wait for me to come for you.'

Then they thought about their son.

'You must make him look like a girl,' said Heinz. 'He's nearly as tall as you. Give him some of your things to wear and a bit of make-up. You can go arm in arm into the Ministeries House. Two new cleaning ladies.'

He fixed a night when there'd be no moon. For once he hoped the weather would be bad. If it was raining there'd be less chance of them being seen. He could only hope.

He had one last job to do. He had to paint his hammer in the paint that would glow. He had to throw the hammer in the dark. His friends would need to find it quickly. The night before his escape he painted the hammer and hid it under the sink in an old rag.

The hours crept by. He did his best to act normally. He went about his jobs as he always did. But his heart was thumping. He imagined the police knocking on his door. He imagined never seeing his family again.

Back at home, school had finished for the day. Heinz's son sat eating his tea in the kitchen.

'I've got something to tell you,' said the boy's mother in a low voice. 'Tonight we're going to escape over the Wall. I don't want you to say a word to anyone. Until we go, act as if everything's normal.'

Her son looked up at her. 'They won't shoot us, will they, Mum?'

She shook her head and made herself smile. 'Don't worry. No one will know until we're safe on the other side. Now I'll tell you what we're going to do . . .'

11

Grey clouds sailed across the dark sky. It was a good time to escape.

In the flat, Heinz's wife got ready. In her bag were her cleaning lady clothes. She'd have to change somewhere on the way to the Ministeries House. She didn't dare risk leaving the flat dressed in different things.

After tea she left the flat with her son. They walked to the park. Hardly anyone was about. They went into some thick bushes to change.

After a few minutes a woman came out. She wore a headscarf, an overall and some flat shoes. What looked like a young girl followed. They walked arm-in-arm out of the park.

The lights were on at the Ministeries House. The cleaners were banging about with brooms and mops. Heinz sat in his room. He felt edgy. He was sanding some wood. If anyone came in it would look as if he was doing his normal work.

His wife and son walked towards the block. Quickly, they went into the building. They could hear the cleaners clanging buckets. The hum of a vacuum cleaner came from one of the rooms.

Heinz had drawn his wife a plan to show her where the lavatory was. She'd remembered the plan in her head. A cleaner came out of a room far down the passage. She was carrying a brush and bucket. She saw Heinz's wife but took no notice.

Now the passage was empty. Using Heinz's key, his wife unlocked the lavatory door. She and her son went in and locked the door behind them. So far, so good. But the 'Out of Order' sign fell to the floor.

They heard footsteps. One of the cleaners tried the door. The sign lay at her feet. She picked it up and tied it back on the door. She walked off, grumbling about having to use the other lavatory. It was on the far side of the building. Her footsteps faded as she walked off. Inside the toilet, Heinz's wife and son held their breath.

After an hour the cleaners put their buckets back in Heinz's workshop and said goodnight. At last, the Ministeries House was quiet. Only Heinz and his family were in the block. And the night caretaker. But the caretaker was in his own room, two floors down. The long passages were dark and full of shadows.

Heinz took out the strong cloth strips his wife had made. He took the three pulleys from the shelf and fixed a strip to each pulley so it made a sort of seat. He took the rope from behind the oil can and the hammer from under the sink. He tied the rope around the hammer. He put the hammer, rope and pulleys into his big tool bag.

At half past midnight he switched off his workshop light and went along the passage. Very quietly he unlocked the lavatory door and let his wife and son out.

They carried their shoes and crept up the stairs to the roof. Heinz opened the roof door and they went out. He locked the door after them.

It was cold. A little rain had begun to fall. He took out the hammer and rope, and the three pulleys with the cloth seats fixed to them. No one spoke. They waited until one o'clock.

On the other side of the Wall his friends had opened a steel box that stood on the street corner. In it were lots of wires. As a clock struck one they cut the wires. The lights that lit up the Wall went out.

The Wall was in darkness.

12

As soon as the lights were out Heinz went to the edge of the roof. He threw the hammer as far as he could. It glowed faintly as it sped over the Wall. He kept hold of the rope which he'd tied around it.

He heard a dull thump as the hammer hit the ground. His friends found it easily and tied a steel cable to it. They gave the hammer a tug. Heinz felt it move and pulled it slowly back up to the roof. The cable came after it.

He fixed the cable to the criss-cross mast. His friends had already fixed the other end. He tested the cable. It was strong and firm.

He put his son's pulley on the cable and lifted him into the cloth seat. He put his legs through the straps so he wouldn't fall out. He kissed him and told him not to be afraid. Then he let him go.

He watched his son glide through the darkness until he was out of sight. Then it was his wife's turn.

When she'd gone Heinz took a last look over the flat roof to the blocks of East Berlin. Faintly, in the distance, came the sound of police sirens.

Quickly he got into his cloth seat. The pulley over his head began to turn. There, on the other side of the Wall, his family were waiting.

The guards thought the lights had fused. They didn't see the cable until morning. By that time Heinz and his friends were having a party.

***

Heinz and his family were lucky. They got away. About 5,000 other people from East Germany also made it. But 60,000 didn't. They were sent to prison for trying to escape. And more than 170 were killed trying to get over the Wall.

Almost 30 years after Heinz made his escape, the Berlin Wall was pulled down. People smashed it to bits with hammers. Crowds from the East flooded into the West. No one could stop them.

And now there is no East Berlin or West Berlin. There is just one city. Berlin. German families split by the Wall are together again.

For the first time since 1961, people can now come and go as they please.

This story was inspired by *True Escape Stories* (Usborne Publishing, 1994).